Once Upon a Starry Sky:

A Reiki Book for Children

By Chantal Marie Cash

Illustrations by: Beatrice Cash

Introduction to Reiki: A Short Guide for Children

This is really for you parents who are either already doing Reiki or are interested in Reiki for a modality for yourselves and or your children. So, this is a very short introduction to Reiki for children. It was a suggestion by a few parents to write this book, and it led me to create this with my own daughter who is also a Reiki practitioner and Reiki Master now.

So, Reiki is not a religion, it is simply put: a way of life. It is a energetic tool that can be implemented into any belief system; it connects you with nature, your soul's purpose, and you will feel the interconnectedness to everything in the Universe. Your belief will have nothing to do with this type of work that you will do with Reiki; and you should encourage your children in the same manner.

I assure all parents, that as we walk into the future with our children, we do not want to make them feel they are divided from us in any way. They will be gifted, and even more so that occasionally we may not understand our children; so Reiki is a tool that will help every child grow into a magnanimous being and wonderful adult human being. A compassionate living soul committed to reconstructing the Earth for our survival— instead of becoming part of the daily grind until we die.

We must teach our children to live; not live in fear. Reiki is also a tool of empowerment, of creating miracles that one can manifest and the abundant possibilities will make one's head spin, truly, but in a fun and good way.

For children, Reiki can be an experience that stretches their imagination and develops their intelligence. Yet, it can also be a healing experience for those who believe in past karmic illness and experiences; and that they do affect us now. Children are far more sensitive than most adults and often remember the past and having had their souls live and die before—this is a way to help alleviate some of the negative effects of karmic influence, as well.

Reiki for children is truly remarkable in the sense that all of their skills; physical and metaphysical will develop accordingly and children will have this tool; this method to increase and create the abilities needed for their future in this life as adults. There are geniuses in all children and Reiki is a way to develop skills naturally, and through the laws of nature and cosmic dispersion Reiki is a constant connection to that energy; which I call Source.

Some children it will come easier to than others—but all can benefit from the basic first level attunement; and many children go on to get the second level as well. It is up to the parents and permission is necessary for me to give the attunements and teach ones children Reiki. Whether, I am the one doing it or not—permission need be granted for the energy exchange to occur.

My oldest went on to become a Reiki Master at 17; it really helps them to develop courage, skills and insights they may not otherwise get until they reach adulthood or even for some until basic life experience has developed. For the average child— why not give them a tool that will help boost their confidence, helps with willingness to learn, and allows one to set measurements of endurance and goals that not only fit their lifestyle—but far surpass any average interests they may have.

In layman's terms—it is a tool that gives children a remarkable advantage—and for those who may be indeed born without a silver spoon in their mouth or may not have other advantages as other children do—this tool creates that possibility. Every child deserves to be happy, healthy and actively engaged in learning about life and all its joys and wonders.

So now, if you feel comfortable with this then it is time to read this book to your children. It is written in poetic rhyme so it is easier for a child to understand. It is written in such a way that is merely conveyed as a simple truth.

This is presented to the world from my inner child to yours. The art was drawn by my daughter who has an advantage since young to be very skilled in some areas—Art, Reading and Writing were but a few; but once she learned Reiki she began to fulfill many of her young childhood dreams.

The truth about Reiki is it is a wonderful guiding tool that can shape a child's reality into a miracle world of wonders. Fulfilling dreams, creating inventions, being authentic are just some of the things gained through use of this energy healing modality.

Since much of the wonders of this are shaped around intention it is wise to teach our children about ethics, behavioral guidelines and of course right and wrong—so that when your child grows they can be compassionate and learn how to be truthful and impeccable souls.

The heart of Reiki is learning compassion and projecting that compassion onto the world—no matter what type of person we are or who we become—it is important to do everything with compassion and joyfulness. Children deserve to be happy, they also deserve to become happy and healthy adults—free from the tyranny of being told who they need to become.

Why not be your own hero and just learn how to live happy and free. That is an essential part of Reiki—now onto the story.

Once upon a starry sky; there were many stars that shone quite bright; inside the space of the night—that held these tiny lights. The star's that sparkle in the night, are shining in the Universe you see—these stars are just one amazing point among one-thousand and one mysteries! This book I hope you enjoy—it will be like no other book or toy. This is for you whether you are a girl or a boy.

Remember that the World and Universe is very old—and much history and stories have been told; about our origins you see—but some of us just know in our hearts what truths we should believe. You my wonderful whimsical child—are about to see the magic behind one of the Universes greatest mysteries!

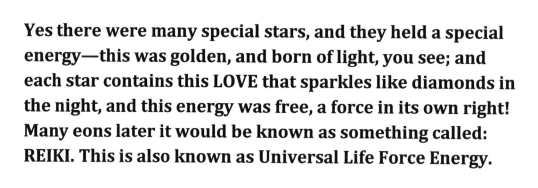

Yes there were many special stars, and they held a special energy—this was golden, and born of light, you see; and each star contains this LOVE that sparkles like diamonds in the night, and this energy was free, a force in its own right! Many eons later it would be known as something called: REIKI. This is also known as Universal Life Force Energy.

So, now my little dear, lend me your ears; for we shall discuss so that there is no fuss. The ONE that people call GOD: created this energy, this force, this beautiful power and love filled mystery. We are the Children of the Sun, and REIKI is that power from the Source of all things; that power cannot be undone—and only joy will it bring. Yes, it can even make your heart, mind, body and soul sing.

Life is like a flower; we bloom brighter day by day—but Reiki just makes us shine and adds colors to our skin like the sun that helps plants to grow—so does REIKI help our spirits growth; and for some of us we get to feel the golden glow. With REIKI; you let the energy flow. That is the first thing that you need to know.

Then, you learn how to harness your own energy; and like a horse in a pasture sometimes you let it run fast and free. Other times you will pull this energy right back in—and yet this Reiki light will never dim. Your light inside your body's chemistry will shine like those stars in the darkest night—remember you are a like a STAR that shines so bright.

So now my little one, think of all your own inner power! Think of Reiki as a golden gentle shower. Think of Reiki as a precious gift; that as you grow makes your consciousness shift. You could become the next Albert Einstein or Vincent Van Gogh, you are unique and indeed a very special soul—that might bring freedom to our human kind—or maybe you will bless the world and make it whole!

Maybe one day you will cure the sick, hurt and the suffering or blind. Imagine my little ones, what Reiki, through YOU can do for all of mankind. Try not to get caught up in that daily grind—as you grow into the amazing adult you will become; don't let your beautiful heart grow numb—you will feel REIKI set you free. You will then understand one of the mysteries.

Imagine too; that you are a magician, a Clown or even a perfect Mathematician. Imagine you can sing, and healing hearts upon command—imagine YOU and is that not grand? Even as a child now—you can see your own future as a grown woman—or man—and you know that the Earth hurts; and so it is time to take a stand. You may just be the one to make the perfect solution or plan.

March with me, little one, and hold out your hand, while I give you the gift of Reiki so you can see the kingdom by the sea—and all its wondrous mysteries. Reiki, can bring into your tiny hearts a power that commands a wilting flower— or puts joy into the homeless man—when you smile at him as you walk by—the joys and triumphs of life can be yours; don't let it pass you by, but please be assured. No soul goes unheard.

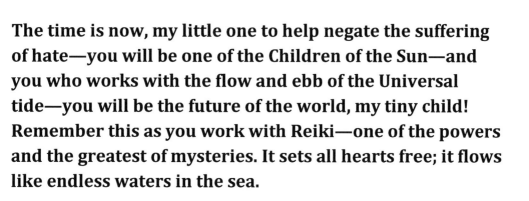

The time is now, my little one to help negate the suffering of hate—you will be one of the Children of the Sun—and you who works with the flow and ebb of the Universal tide—you will be the future of the world, my tiny child! Remember this as you work with Reiki—one of the powers and the greatest of mysteries. It sets all hearts free; it flows like endless waters in the sea.

So now let me explain, a little bit for you about how Reiki can benefit your young life, and what stage it sets for you, and as you grow you will be given more clues. If you work with it every day—you will see amazing things, come what may. The miracle that you seek will keep you from becoming weak. The joys of life will compel you to learn, and in you will be a passion for learning that burns. Good things that REIKI brings—yes, it will truly make your young heart sing!

So Reiki is an energy that when used creates great change; though some people think it is quite strange. Intention is at the heart, remember that from the start. Once you receive a magical initiation called an attunement, you really get to see the miracles happen. It is a blessing that never passes. You will feel confident among the masses—and who knows maybe you will even excel in your classes.

One day, you can become a Reiki Master; and this is what the world needs to avoid impending disasters. Men like Tesla, could have saved the world, and how many think he was quite absurd. Inside you hold the keys to the kingdom—so let us unlock the codes and all young lives are here to change the fate of the world—I assure you that you know that is not absurd. The youth are the future, not the past—and REIKI is a healing method set to last.

Now young child, what would you like to grow up to be? Controlled by fate: or a Master of your own destiny? Which would you rather be? Reiki can be sent to the future or the past—it is going to be one tool to help at long last. Imagine a world where people created their needs being met out of thin air—well, REIKI almost has that energetic flare. Reiki will make you smile inside—it will also manifest miracles and from the world you will not hide. No time to be shy, no time to fear; I promise you this child—Reiki makes you feel more courageous and clear.

Remember that intention creates the change—thought goes where energy flows—this is how the Universe works in all its joys and wonders and quirks. Be blissful, is the motto of REIKI—be kind to others, do not be angry in your heart, do not worry, do your work and fight for truth—what more diligence can you find then in youth? Be kind to every living thing—this is a motto that kindness does bring—it brings us to be centered in our hearts and to be victors from the start.

To be a child that grows into a woman or a man; and understands the greater plan—that is the wisdom that is at the heart of Reiki—and of course the brilliant fractals of energy—that will fill up your heart and mind—So now as you think about what has been placed into your hands; an energetic light so bright that it can illuminate even the darkest night. Now while you think of how wonderful you are, like those tiny distant stars...please think about the energy that I give from me to thee.

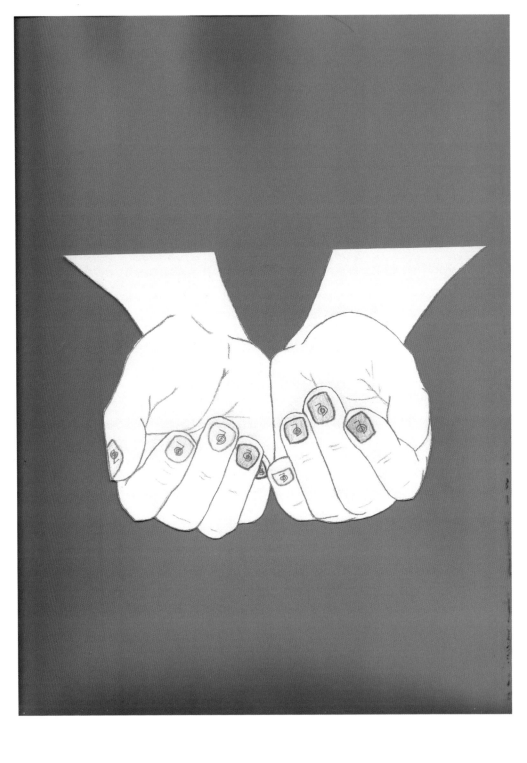

So now my child, if you who wish to be attuned, listen now for the pulse from the Mother Earth—can you hear nature as it gives birth and self-worth to every living thing. Yes, this is an awareness that Reiki can bring. Do you feel the life on the ocean floors, or the birds in the trees; do you feel the breath of life in the wind blowing through the leaves; do you my young friend I implore! Do you feel the power symbol blowing through the doors of your crown—this energy is golden and loving and re-known!

Reiki sings into the heart of nature; it also makes you feel extremely grateful. You learn to lose fear you learn how to care. Sometimes you get to learn things you always wanted to do and always it keeps you connected to truth. My young souls far and wide—take up Reiki and let it be your guide. Let this force up lift you and you will feel connected to the almighty presence; this is the Source of the Universal Essence.

My young friends God lives in your heart; this is the connection to the original God from the start; and Reiki has always been connected to that wondrous power—and you will become like a golden yellow -flower—and as the energy of Reiki flows through you like a beautiful dream and you use it for what it is truly worth; one day you will understand that promise given long before the moment of your birth. This is part of the great mystery, and as a child that sees; I attest this to thee.

My Child, you will learn this tool and as it helps you learn and grow; you will create better seeds to sew. You will fight for truth with all your might; and you will feel like that star that shines so brightly in the night. Imagine my child, what you can now do—imagine this as you hold onto your youth. Never forget the magic inside—always let your inner child be your guide. Reiki is a tool like a rattle to a babe—and one day many hearts you will save.

I hope you learned about Reiki today—I feel confident you will enjoy learning and growing and never forget to play—regardless of what follows you to the end of your days. May the sky and the sun and the moon and the stars—may the gift of Creation carry you far. The light in the heavens unto you will shine—may the gift of Reiki give you energy and fill you with light—yes may this gift raise you up and allow you to shine—as you grow into your body— you will watch as your heart and soul align.

The End

Afterword

As I said, at the request of many parents this was written for the benefit of children. As a teacher of Reiki I feel it is crucial that our future generations learn this energetic modality. I also feel that when families learn this together, and this was suggested by a client, friend and mentor as well—at her request she said; "You will be writing a book for children on Reiki—you better get on that!" I was like, well okay, yes I have been thinking about it for some time.

I needed an artist; that was the main issue. So my daughter has used her artistic gifts and with the help of Reiki she did an excellent job depicting nature and the story through her creative illustrations. We are both very excited to share this with you and your child or children.

It is important that if you want the Reiki attunement for your child or children and of course that it is something they want as well—then consider this book the introduction to their training. This short little concise poetic book is for the innocent child who wishes to learn—they have as much right to learn about this as anyone.

Imagine a child between the ages of 5 to 10; this being a time in their lives where imagination is also playing the part of teacher. So Reiki stimulates not only this part of the brain, but also other aspects of cognitive function, including the development of abilities or traits that can greatly enhance their life in many positive ways.

Before Reiki I felt something was missing from my life—again let me stress this is not Religion, but can be used in accordance with your personal belief system. Encourage your children to think for themselves—do not tell them what to believe in instead show them how grateful you are for their unique individual nature and how blessed you are to call them your child or children, and they will equally respond and be grateful that "you" are their parent(s).

Such a natural thing as connecting to Universal Life Force Energy is crucial to our understanding many things outside the scope of what we were taught in schools, by our parents, church and government. If you are interested in learning this energy modality then you may contact me or another Reiki Master. It is important when having your children attuned you do not go to just anyone; ask about their training and whatever questions you have of them to make sure that Teacher is of the highest quality for you and your children.

I may be reached at lightnbliss@live.com or you may visit my website at: www.freewebs.com/pathwaystowellness this has much of what I do addressed on the site. I enjoy teaching Reiki to families; so if you would like this service it does not matter if you are local or long distance attunements and classes are available upon request.

Biography of Beatrice Cash; RMT

I have been aware of Reiki since my childhood days and have attained Reiki Master Status, thanks to my Mom and other mentors. Most everybody uses it to help other people but I prefer to use it with animals. It really does seem to help them, especially to alleviate pain or discomfort, or even if you just want to feel closer to any specific animal.

I've even been able to coax chipmunks onto my lap, have them eat right out of my hand! I've always been into the natural world around us, animals, plants and nature. I even live up in the middle of nowhere, where my closest neighbors are the variety of squirrels, rabbits, birds, bears and deer that frequently roam throughout my land.

I can say that I have truly witnessed and done some wonderful things because of Reiki. The one thing I will always remember is visiting the wolf sanctuary out in Colorado, and how one of the wolves came right up to me, placed her paws on my lap, stared into my eyes and gave me a big old French kiss.

Throughout the whole experience my heart was pounding so hard and I stayed perfectly still. I wasn't frightened, because I knew that she wouldn't hurt me, but it's important to have respect for something that sentient, that wild and potentially dangerous and I can say that it is all thanks to Reiki.

I am ready now to do what I was brought here to do, and have discovered wondrous things about myself, nature and others that I may not have had access to understanding before the Reiki attunements. I am forever grateful for this experience as it has enhanced my life in so many ways.

Biography of Chantal Cash; CH & RMT

I was born in Minnesota and has lived there much of my life. My mother was from the Netherlands, and my father's side, though American, were from Bavaria and Wales. As a child I suffered several traumas. When I was small I was always interested in fairies and Angels. I was always looking for ways to fix things without going to the doctor and I worked with many aspects of myself.

Being the single mother of four children, I was ready to take out a new lease on life. I began looking into all avenues of natural healing. I was sick and tired of being 'sick and tired'. I was in a pre-obese state, I had Hashimoto Thyroiditis. I was angry and was in need of a life changing experience. So I began by taking vitamins, supplements and changing my eating habits. My biggest problem back then was my weight. So I began looking into fast and easy remedies. The one that really helped me was Hypnosis. This though, did not satisfy my curiosity. I then decided to become a Hypnotist.

I took Cal Banyans 5 Path program and became a Certified Hypnotist. I also am a 7th Path Instructor which is the Self-

Hypnosis program he teaches, and this was first and foremost the starting point for me. This is what kept me hooked to my weight loss. Hypnosis took me personally and professionally into a new direction. By this time having gotten my physical and emotional health in order, I then moved onto spirit.

By the time I was 32 I knew about love and kindness, but it took a lot of rough patches to feel how far I had really gotten in this life. I saw that compassion moved mountains in my life and that of others. I began to look for ways to change my Spiritual health. I had been raised Catholic and I had been exposed to varying religions over the years; I began to pursue alternatives to Religion.

To be honest, it was hard for me to believe and I never took things at face value. I started to meditate, work with stones and essential oils; I took up a daily prayer practice. This of course eventually put me in the path of Reiki. Since I wanted a true relationship with Source, I started to do research in the different types of energy healing. I started by receiving Reiki from Stephani Brail. I then went on to look at various teachers. I found Shaman Maggie Wahls and took her classes: Level One and Two: Usui Reiki and her Shamanism classes.

Later on, I then took classes from a local instructor Jodi Tschida to receive my Usui Reiki Master and Teacher levels. It did not take long and I found that I was waking up one day to discover that I could do things I never used to be able to do. I woke up one morning after just starting to read a book on Crystals and

Minerals. The next morning, after reading only two or three chapters, I knew (inspiringly) all about the stones.

I then began to take other classes introducing myself to Aromatherapy and eventually taking a class to become an Essential Oil Raindrop Specialist. I began practicing telepathy. I began to communicate with spirits and see peoples past lives imprinted on them. I established a relationship with my guides and Angels, and eventually it led me to communication with the Divine or Source as I prefer to say.

For the first time I really began to see LIFE for the wonder it really was. All areas of Natural Medicine had been put into my path. I was eager to learn and applied myself where I thought I could be of the most help. Other areas of interest I have acquired and incorporated into my business are: Crystal stone Layouts, Dowsing and Reiki; classes and sessions, Tarot readings and Oracle readings, Jewelry making and other crafts, to name just a few.

In my spare time I write poetry and other literary works, make scrap books, garden, I read and do research for my work. I have four children: two daughters and two sons. My sons have Autism. I am a support manager for a Non-profit company that enables disabled people to lead more independent lives. I work with my sons and have worked with other Autistic children and Adults. I find this work to be extremely rewarding. I enjoy my job very much.

In addition, I have four businesses. I have created these businesses as a way of reaching out to people in these varying avenues of interest. I also am working on finishing my Associates in Criminal Justice, though that has been placed on the back burner for now. I would like to do non-Profit work as an Advocate to serve those who experience social injustice. Specifically: focusing in the areas of the develop mentally disabled; and to continue my work with Autistic persons. In any of my sessions my focus is Mind body Spirit connection. In any of my businesses I utilize all my tools and I use any knowledge I have to help my family, my clients, friends, and community.

New Perceptions Hypnosis & Reiki is my first business that I opened in 2007. I then incorporated the Reiki into my first business as well. Inner Chi Crystal Jewelry and Chi KI Arts & Crafts are catered around spiritually made gifts and other handmade items.

In addition, I have MAOM: this is an acronym for Metaphysical Association of Minnesota. This business focuses on people who are having spiritual issues or are in need of guidance due to a haunting, spiritual attack or other supernatural occurrence. I specialize in assisting people to invoke a higher spiritual awareness and when necessary I do spirit releasement therapy known as SRT through Hypnosis or I make house calls to assist the client in removing and cleansing property, the people that live there and their pets.

The aspect about the work that I love the most is reaching out to people and assisting them in their goals towards health and healing, be it: Emotional, Physical or Spiritual. Working with Source daily helps me to be creative in all areas of my life. I enjoy being a Co-Creator with Source. I work with The Earth, the elements, the Universe, the all in all. I am excited to teach people about Reiki and Self-Hypnosis and to help them learn how to explore their past, to embrace their present and look forward to their future.

In addition I have been writing for many years. Specifically, short stories, fiction, poetry and of course self- help/self- trans- formation informative guiding works. I am the author of the book on Dowsing, Totems, Reiki and much more. I am interested in many metaphysical topics: and write about those varying issues and topics that people come to me for through teaching Hypnosis or Reiki—my interests are many and truly are not limited.

I enjoy writing in my spare time and it has become very important to me to write daily. I feel that the negative experiences from my childhood helped to transform me into the person that I am today. I believe that knowing what I know now, we can transform our worries, our fears and even our traumas into something positive. Reiki has changed my life— without this energy and direct access to Source I would not have made it this far—of that I am most certain. The God Spark is in us all—but to ignite it to its full passion is what I did and my daughter too—we pushed it to the limit and we broke the mold.

Brightest of blessings to you, and to your children.

In Light, Unity and Truth,

Chantal Cash and Beatrice Cash

26743511R00028

Printed in Great Britain
by Amazon